I0707734

THE COMPLEX CHALLENGES OF

PAN AFRICANISM

THE IDEOLOGY AND THE REALITY

A VELI MABONA BOOK

©Mabona2024

Table of Content:

Background

This list below enumerates the world's poorest countries in 2024, with a specific focus on African nations. The following African countries are included in the list, along with their rankings and GDP-PPP per capital:

Source: Global Finance Magazine
gfmag.com/data/economic-data/poorest-country-in-the-world/

RANK	Country	GDP-PPP per capita ($)
1	South Sudan	455
2	Burundi	916
3	Central African Republic	1,123
4	Democratic Republic of the Congo	1,552
5	Mozambique	1,649
6	Niger	1,675
7	Malawi	1,712
8	Liberia	1,882
9	Madagascar	1,979
11	Somalia	2,062
12	Sierra Leone	2,189
13	Chad	2,620
15	Mali	2,714
16	Burkina Faso	2,781
17	Togo	2,911

19	Zimbabwe	2,975
20	The Gambia	2,993
22	Lesotho	3,227
23	Guinea-Bissau	3,239
24	Uganda	3,345
25	Guinea	3,366
26	Rwanda	3,367
27	Sudan	3,443
28	Comoros	3,532
31	Tanzania	3,746
33	Ethiopia	4,020
35	Zambia	4,361
36	Benin	4,558
37	Senegal	4,661
39	Republic of Congo	4,740
40	Cameroon	4,842
46	Nigeria	6,340
49	Ivory Coast	6,860
51	Kenya	6,976
52	Angola	7,153
53	Ghana	7,156
54	Tonga	7,462
68	Morocco	10,947
72	Namibia	12,008
76	Eswatini	12,637
78	Tunisia	13,645
85	South Africa	16, 424
86	Algeria	16,483
93	Egypt	17,614
95	Equatorial Guinea	18,378

99	Gabon	19,452
104	Botswana	**20,097**
118	Libya	**26,456**
126	**Mauritius**	**32,094**

Top ten Diamond producing countries in the world 2024.

Source: ADDA 24.7 Current Affairs currentaffairs.adda247.com/top-10-diamonds-producing-countries-in-the-world

RANK	Country	Diamond Production (Carats)
1	Russia	41,923,910
2	**Botswana**	**24,752,967**
3	Canada	16,249,218
4	**Democratic Republic of Congo**	**9,908,998**
5	**South Africa**	**9,660,233**
6	**Angola**	**8,763,309**
7	**Zimbabwe**	**4,461,450**
8	**Namibia**	**2,054,227**
9	**Lesotho**	**727,737**
10	**Sierra Leone**	**688,970**

Top five leading countries based on mine production of platinum worldwide in 2023.

Source: Statista.com

statista.com/statistics

RANK	Country	In metric tons
1	**South Africa**	41,923,910
2	Russia	24,752,967
3	**Zimbabwe**	16,249,218
4	Canada	9,908,998
5	United States	9,660,233
6	Other countries	8,763,309

Top eight largest producers of cobalt-producing countries in the world 2021.

Source: NS Energy

nsenergybusiness.com/analysis/top-cobalt-producing-countries?cf-view

RANK	Country	Tonnes
1	**Democratic Republic of Congo**	**100 000**
2	Russia	6100
3	Australia	5100
4	Philippines	4600
5	Cuba	3500
6	**Madagascar**	**3300**
7	Papua New Guinea	3100
8	Canada	3000

Top ten largest producers of copper-producing countries in the world 2021.

Source: VisualCapitalist.com
visualcapitalist.com/visualizing-the-worlds-largest/copper-producers/

RANK	Country	Million Tonnes
1	Chile	5.6
2	Peru	2.2
3	China	1.8
4	**Democratic Republic of Congo**	**1.8**
5	United States	1.2
6	Australia	0.9
7	Russia	0.8
8	**Zambia**	**0.8**
9	Indonesia	0.8
10	Mexico	0.7

The number of coups that have happened in Africa since 1950

Source: Voice of America

projects.voanews.com/African-coups/

Country	Total attempts	Successful
Sudan	18	6
Burundi	11	5
Burkina Faso	10	9
Ghana	10	5
Sierra Leone	10	5
Comoros	9	4
Guinea-Bissau	9	4
Benin	8	6
Nigeria	8	6
Togo	7	3
Republic of Congo	7	2
Chad	7	2
Mauritania	7	5
Guinea	6	3
Ethiopia	5	2
Central African Republic	5	3
Uganda	5	3
Egypt	4	4
Democratic Republic of Congo	4	2
Algeria	4	2
Madagascar	4	1

Liberia	4	1
Lesotho	4	3
Ivory Coast	4	1
Somalia	3	1
Gabon	3	1
Libya	3	1
Zambia	3	0
The Gambia	3	1
Sao Tome	3	1
Equatorial Guinea	2	1
Morocco	2	0
Rwanda	2	2
Senegal	1	0
Mozambique	1	0
Angola	1	0
Seychelles	1	1
Kenya	1	1
Eswatini	1	1
Cameroon	1	0
Tunisia	1	1
Djibouti	1	0
Zimbabwe	1	1

Ten African countries with the highest number of languages

Source: Adekunle Agbetiloye
Africa.business.com/local/lifestyle/10-African-countries-with-the-highest-number-of-languages/

RANK	Country	Number of languages
1	**Nigeria**	520
2	**Cameroon**	227
3	**Democratic Republic of Congo**	214
4	**Chad**	129
5	**Tanzania**	128
6	**Ethiopia**	92
7	**Ivory Coast**	88
8	**Ghana**	83
9	**Sudan**	75
10	**South Sudan**	73

Major ethnic groups

Source:

en.wikipedia.org/wiki/list_of_ethnic_groups_of_Africa

Major Ethnic groups	Region	Countries
Akan	West Africa	Ghana, Ivory Coast
Amhara	Horn of Africa	Ethiopia
Arabs	North Africa	Algeria, Libya, Morocco, Tunisia, Mauritania
Berbers	North Africa	Algeria, Libya, Morocco, Mauritania
Chewa	Central Africa	Malawi, Zambia
Fulani	West Africa	Mauritania, Gambia, Guinea-Bissau, Guinea, Nigeria, Cameroon, Senegal, Mali, Burkina Faso, Benin, Niger, Chad, Sudan, Central African Republic, Ghana,

		Togo, Sierra Leone
Hausa	West Africa	Nigeria, Niger, Benin, Ghana, Cameroon, Chad, Sudan
Hutu	Central Africa	Rwanda, Burundi, Democratic Republic of the Congo
Igbo	West Africa	Nigeria, Equatorial Guinea, Cameroon, Gabon
Kanuri	Central Africa	Nigeria Niger Chad Cameroon
Kongo	Central Africa	Democratic Republic of the Congo, Angola, Republic of the Congo
Luba	Central Africa	Democratic Republic of the Congo

Mongo	Central Africa	Democratic Republic of the Congo
Mossi	West Africa	Burkina Faso, Ivory Coast, Niger, Ghana, Mali, Togo
Nilotes	Nile Valley, East Africa, Central Africa	South Sudan, Sudan, Chad, Central African Republic, Kenya, Uganda, Tanzania, Ethiopia
Oromo	Horn of Africa	Ethiopia, Kenya
Shona	Southern Africa	Zimbabwe and Mozambique
Somali	Horn of Africa	Somalia, Djibouti, Ethiopia, Kenya
Songhai	West Africa	Niger, Mali, Burkina Faso, Nigeria, Algeria
Yoruba	West Africa	Nigeria, Benin, Togo, Ghana, Ivory Coast, Sierra Leone
Zulu	Southern Africa	South Africa

List of Bantu Peoples by Country

Source: en.wikipedia.org/wiki/Bantu-peoples

Country	Total population (millions, 2015 est)	Bantu groups
Democratic Republic of the Congo	77	Bakongo, Mongo, Baluba, numerous others (Ambala, Ambuun, Angba, Babindi, Baboma, Baholo, Balunda, Bangala, Bango, Batsamba, Bazombe, Bemba, Bembe, Bira, Bowa, Dikidiki, Dzing, Fuliiru, Havu, Hema, Hima, Hunde, Hutu, Iboko, Kanioka, Kaonde, Kuba, Komo, Kwango, Lengola, Lokele, Lupu, Lwalwa, Mbala, Mbole, Mbuza (Budja), Nande, Ngoli, Bangoli, Ngombe, Nkumu, Nyanga, Bapende, Popoi, Poto, Sango, Shi, Songo, Sukus, Tabwa, Tchokwé, Téké, Tembo, Tetela, Topoke, Ungana, Vira, Wakuti, Nyindu, Yaka, Yakoma, Yanzi, Yeke, Yela, total 80% Bantu)

Tanzania		51	Abakuria, Sukuma, Nyamwezi, Haya, Chaga, Gogo, Makonde, Ngoni, Matumbi, numerous others (majority Bantu)
South Africa		55	Nguni (Zulu, Hlubi, Xhosa, Southern Ndebele, Swazi), Basotho (South Sotho), Bapedi (North Sotho), Venda, Batswana, Tsonga, Kgaga (North Sotho),[59] total 75% Bantu
Kenya		46	Agikuyu, Abaluhya, ABASUBA, Akamba, Abagusii, Ameru, Abakuria, Aembu, Ambeere, Taita, Pokomo, Taveta and Mijikenda, numerous others (60% Bantu)
Mozambique		28	Makua, Sena, Shona (Ndau), Shangaan (Tsonga), Makonde, Yao, Swahili, Tonga, Chopi, Ngoni
Uganda		37	Baganda, Basoga, Bagwere, Banyoro, Banyankole, Bakiga, Batooro, Bamasaba, Basamia, Bakonjo, Baamba, Baruuli, Banyole, Bafumbira, Bagungu (majority Bantu)
Angola		26	Ovimbundu, Ambundu, Bakongo, Bachokwe,

		Balunda, Ganguela, Ovambo, Herero, Xindonga (97% Bantu)
Malawi	16	Chewa, Tumbuka, Yao, Lomwe, Sena, Tonga, Ngoni, Ngonde
Zambia	15	Nyanja-Chewa, Bemba, Tonga, Tumbuka, BaLunda, Balovale, Kaonde, Nkoya and Lozi, about 70 groups total.
Zimbabwe	14	Shona, Northern Ndebele, Bakalanga, numerous minor groups.
Rwanda	11	Banyarwanda
Burundi	10	Barundi
Cameroon	22	Bulu, Duala, Ewondo, Bafia Bassa, Bakoko, Barombi, Mbo, Subu, Bakwe, Oroko, Bafaw, Fang, Bekpak, Mbam speakers 30% Bantu
Republic of the Congo	5	Bakongo, Sangha, Mbochi, Bateke, Bandzabi, Bapunu, Bakuni, Bavili, Batsangui, Balari, Babémbé, Bayaka, Badondo, Bayaka, Bahumbu.
Botswana	2.2	Batswana, BaKalanga, Mayeyi 90% Bantu
Equatorial Guinea	2.0	Fang, Bubi, 95% Bantu
Lesotho	1.9	Basotho

Gabon	1.9	Fang, Nzebi, Myene, Kota, Shira, Punu, Kande.
Namibia	2.3	Ovambo, Kavango, Herero, Himba, Mayeyi 70% Bantu
Eswatini	1.1	Swazi, Zulu, Tsonga
Somalia	13.8	Somali Bantu, Bajuni
Comoros	0.8	Somali Bantu, BajuniComorian people

Preface

"Africans are sort of lazy people...when I go to Africa, I am very down... I don't get fantastic vibes from the people; I am just really bored"
Tina Turner

The passing of Tina Turner marked a poignant moment for me as a devoted fan who had cherished her music, particularly from the iconic Ike and Tina Turner era. My immediate response was to express my grief on various social network platforms, seeking comfort in the virtual community of fellow admirers. However, amidst the collective mourning, an old interview resurfaced, featuring Turner expressing disparaging views about the African continent. Reacting instinctively, I strongly rebuked her statements, quickly deleting any posts that glorified her. Yet, as the emotional confusion settled in the weeks that followed, I found myself compelled to revisit her comments with a more open perspective. Upon reflection, I grappled with the uncomfortable realisation that, perhaps, Turner's assessment of Africa wasn't entirely unfounded. She candidly depicted a continent damaged by extensive issues, including poverty, corruption, and internal conflicts manifesting as self-inflicted sabotage amongst its people. I look at Africa as a metaphorical ghetto, a space fraught with insecurity, where one repeatedly senses the looming vision of victimhood and statistical unimportance. This portrayal resonated with the disheartening reality of a continent grappling with challenges that have, to a significant extent, hindered its development and unity. In contemplating Turner's remarks, I became acutely aware of the uncomfortable truths she highlighted about Africa's socio-political landscape. Acknowledging these harsh realities prompted a critical self-examination of my initial emotional response. This journey of introspection compelled me to transcend the instinctual reaction and engage in a more enlightened exploration of the continent's complexities, recognising the necessity for a candid discourse on Africa's challenges while also envisioning pathways toward positive transformation.

Over the past few years, my professional journey has afforded me the privilege of working within an academic institution, where I have encountered brilliant minds deeply engaged in the emergent trend of embracing decolonial scholarship and advocating for Pan-Africanism. My involvement includes organising conferences and events that focus on decoloniality and Pan-Africanist ideologies. However, my experiences have prompted critical observations regarding the authenticity of the commitment among some decolonial leaders. Unfortunately, a portion of these figures appears more infatuated with the perks of privilege, such as business-class travel and luxurious accommodations, than with a genuine belief in the principles they espouse, particularly the vision of a unified Africa. The conferences and events I've been a part of have often fallen short in generating practical solutions. Financial resources are poured into explorations of historical criticisms, primarily placing blame on external entities like white people, Europe, and the United States, with the Berlin Conference singled out as a convenient scapegoat for Africa's contemporary challenges. Regrettably, the romanticised notion of a united Africa impedes substantive progress. The truth, historically grounded, asserts that Africa, like any continent with a rich civilization, had distinct borders outlining clans and a system of land claims. The reality is that Africa was never a homogeneously united continent, with tribes and nations using natural features like lakes, rivers, and mountains as markers of territorial boundaries. To foster prosperity on the African continent, a shift towards self-accountability is imperative. Acknowledging that internal conflicts, wars, betrayal, and self-serving leadership are predominantly homegrown issues is essential. Contrary to popular Pan-Africanist and Black Consciousness ideologies, which originated in the diaspora's fight for equality and civil rights, the struggle in Africa has historically centred on land issues rather than a quest for equality. Furthermore, the continent's inclination to embrace foreign ideologies, whether Pan-Africanism, Communism, or Capitalism, rather than formulating indigenous systems, contributes to a deep-seated internal division. In essence, the responsibility for Africa's challenges lies squarely with its inhabitants, necessitating a collective effort to overcome these internal obstacles. The historical context of conquest and colonisation is not unique to Africa but deeply ingrained in the human psyche across continents. In Europe, every nation has undergone episodes of conquest and colonization, echoing a similar trend in Asia, with Japan being the only nation that evaded colonization. What distinguishes Africa from other continents is the way societies have processed and transcended their historical legacies. While Europe and Asia have found ways to move forward, evolving into new societies and maintaining historical records, Africa appears to be grappling with a persistent attachment to its past. The continent seems stuck in a historical narrative that hinders evolution and progress, a stark contrast to the adaptive paths observed elsewhere. Crucially, Africa must confront the reality of its conquest and colonization, acknowledging the transformative impact these periods have had on its social fabric. The emphasis must shift from dwelling on the divisive elements rooted in tribalism and religious differences imposed during the conquest era to a collective acceptance that the continent has endured significant historical shifts. It is imperative for Africa to acknowledge its past, recognizing the centuries-long struggle for freedom, and transition into a phase of collective evolution.

The academic landscape in Africa, however, reflects a continued influence of European thought. The dominance of European scholars in shaping academic discourse, the reliance on European teaching methodologies, and the prevalence of Christianity and decolonial perspectives among academics underscore a lingering influence that impedes the formulation of authentically African academic agendas. Moreover, the pursuit of luxury and status symbols among scholars suggests a disconnect between academic pursuits and a true commitment to advancing indigenous knowledge systems. For Africa to move forward, there must be a deliberate effort to decolonize academic spaces, fostering a more balanced and authentic representation of African perspectives and methodologies. Only through such introspection and transformation can the continent truly emancipate itself from the shadows of its colonial past and chart a course towards a self-determined future. One significant factor hindering the unification of Africa is the prevalence of witchcraft, or dark magic. Although I will not dedicate an entire chapter to this matter due to the lack of scientific proof or practical data, it warrants mention in the introduction. Initially, I considered omitting this topic from the book, but if theologians can discuss and write about God without scientific evidence, relying solely on faith, then addressing witchcraft is similarly justified. Whether one believes in dark magic or not, the reality is that protection against it has become a billion-dollar industry. Upon close inspection, the foundation of witchcraft often lies in individuals who feel they cannot progress in life. Rather than seeking solutions to improve their own circumstances, they invest time and effort in attempting to send bad luck and grab good fortune from successful people. The underlying logic is that the presence of successful individuals around them intensifies their own feelings of failure, leading them to prefer a scenario where everyone remains on the same level. This obsession with dark magic and the concerted effort to hinder others' progress pose significant obstacles to unity. It is challenging to foster a sense of collective advancement when individuals are preoccupied with sabotaging each other's success. In many workplaces, witchcraft is prevalent, with individuals attempting to disrupt healthy relationships and professional progress.

Alarmingly, those who engage in these practices are often family members, neighbours, friends, and colleagues, which further complicates efforts to build trust and unity within communities. Addressing the impact of witchcraft on societal cohesion is crucial for understanding one of the unique challenges Africa faces in its quest for unity. Recognizing and confronting this cultural phenomenon is essential to fostering an environment where collective progress is possible, and where individuals can support one another's success without fear of malicious interference.

1

Read between the lines!

I recently attended a Pan Africanist symposium where one of the speakers was the brilliant Professor Tshepo Madlingozi. In his presentation, Professor Madlingozi spoke about various great revolutionaries who fought against colonization. One of the revolutionaries he highlighted was Doman, a legendary Khoikhoi leader. Initially, Doman worked with the Dutch East India Company (VOC) as an interpreter. His role afforded him a unique position within the Dutch colonial structure. However, a significant turning point in Doman's life occurred when the VOC took him to Java. During his time in Java, Doman witnessed firsthand the harsh treatment and exploitation the VOC inflicted upon the native Javanese people. This exposure profoundly impacted Doman, revealing to him the true nature of the colonial enterprise and the oppressive force behind the VOC's operations. Upon his return to Cape Town, Doman's viewpoint had permanently shifted. Armed with the knowledge and insight gained from his experience in Java, he became a avid opponent of the Dutch colonizers. He organized and led a revolt against the Dutch in Cape Town, employing guerrilla tactics and strategic raids. Doman and his followers achieved several successful raids against the Dutch, demonstrating their resilience and tactical acumen. Despite their successes, Doman's forces faced significant challenges. The most formidable of these was the Castle of Good Hope, a stronghold that the Khoikhoi were unable to storm successfully. Doman's story took a tragic turn when he was eventually injured, leading to the crushing of the rebellion he spearheaded. Despite the initial success in guerrilla raids against the Dutch, the uprising ultimately failed to dislodge the colonizers. In the aftermath, peace talks ensued, and Doman returned to working with the Dutch East India Company. Sadly, he died shortly thereafter, marking the end of a significant yet ultimately unsuccessful chapter of resistance. Reflecting on Doman's tale, I found myself contemplating the contemporary status of the

Khoisan people. This thought will be revisited later.

At the Pan Africanist symposium, I was, as always, struck by the sheer intellectual weight present in the room. The Pan Africanist movement has a unique ability to draw in some of the brightest minds, creating an intimidating atmosphere for someone like me. Unlike many attendees, I do not come from an academic background. Instead, I have grown up immersed in politics, actively participated in political activities, and led branches. My expertise lies in practical politics, both local and international.

As I observed the audience, I was astounded by the unwavering belief in and commitment to the Pan Africanist ideology among these intellectuals. It was a revelation to see these scholars, with their profound academic backgrounds, dedicated to realizing this ideology. However, a striking observation was the apparent disconnect between these intellectual giants and the general populace. These scholars, despite their brilliance, often find it challenging to communicate their ideas in a way that resonates with the everyday person. This gap between intellectual discourse and public understanding presents a significant obstacle for the Pan Africanist movement. The challenge lies in bridging this gap, translating complex ideological concepts into accessible narratives that can mobilize the broader community. Only by making this ideology comprehensible and relevant to the average individual can the movement gain the widespread support necessary for its success. I completely understand the motivation behind the diaspora advocating for a Pan Africanist ideology. However, I find it confusing when scholars from this continent genuinely embrace Pan Africanism. This confusion led to the initial title of my book, which aggressively labelled Pan Africanists as fools; a title I subsequently changed out of respect for some of the most brilliant individuals I know. Nonetheless, my fundamental contention remains. I don't understand how academic who have lived in Africa all their lives, cannot recognize that Africans are inherently resistant to unity? Our deeply ingrained pride, distinct identities, and egos serve as formidable barriers to such unity. The unfortunate reality is that Africa consistently lags when it comes to timing and seizing critical historical moments. The process of nation building is basically tied to conflict and bloodshed, and often demands uncompromising resolve. Historically, it requires generations of conquest before conquered peoples can fully integrate and live in unity. This harsh truth underscores the complexity of uniting a continent as diverse and fragmented as Africa. Pan Africanism, as a theoretical idea, may hold significant appeal and offer a vision of solidarity and collective progress. However, the practical implementation of this ideology faces immense challenges. The historical, cultural, and social fabric of Africa is woven with a host of ethnicities, languages, and traditions. These differences, while enriching the continent, also create substantial hurdles to achieving the kind of unity Pan Africanism envisions. Moreover, the political landscape in many African countries is marked by corruption, nepotism, and a struggle for power, further complicating efforts to advance unity. The aspiration for a united Africa, must contend with these deeply rooted issues. Building nations requires not only visionary leadership but also the willingness to endure and navigate through periods of intense conflict and transformation. It is a path fraught with challenges, demanding both patience and an unwavering commitment to the long-term goal of unity.

Let us now turn our attention back to the Khoisan people. The Khoisan are particularly intriguing to me because they embody both the Pan Africanist theory of uniting to survive and my own theory of surviving through nationalism while maintaining cordial relations with neighbours. Historically, the Khoisan people were displaced from their territories by both Bantu groups and white colonizers. Despite their rich heritage and longstanding presence in the region, the Khoisan have not reclaimed their ancestral lands. According to contemporary national borders and concepts of territoriality, the entire region of Southern Africa originally belongs to the San. In today's South Africa, the Khoisan face significant marginalization. None of their languages hold official status in the country, and their representation in parliament is insufficient. This lack of recognition and representation underscores the systemic neglect they experience. Many Khoisan individuals have integrated into what is now referred to as the Coloured community, losing much of their distinct cultural identity in the process. Those who have managed to retain their Khoisan identity often live in conditions of poverty and face high levels of unemployment. The plight of the Khoisan people illustrates the complex interplay between historical displacement and contemporary struggles for recognition and rights. Their situation serves as a poignant reminder of the broader challenges facing indigenous populations in post-colonial Africa. Despite the significant contributions of the Khoisan to the cultural and historical tapestry of Southern Africa, they remain on the margin of socio-economic and political life. This sidelining highlights the need for a more inclusive approach to nation building, one that acknowledges and integrates the diverse cultural and historical legacies of all peoples. The Khoisan's experience suggests that survival and progress in modern Africa require not only unity and nationalism but also a commitment to justice and rightful representation. As Bantu Africans, it is confusing why we are seemingly content about the fact that the Khoisan people were conquered, and that the vast lands and minerals of Southern Africa, which originally belonged to them, are now under our domination. We have accepted their status as a conquered people without much reflection. This acceptance contrasts sharply with our persistent preoccupation with our own history of colonization and suffering under foreign rule. The gap in our responses to these two historical injustices raises critical questions about our collective memory and moral consistency. While we continuously highlight and lament the colonial suppression of our ancestors, we often overlook the prior displacement and sidelining of the Khoisan. This selective historical awareness may reflect underlying biases and a reluctance to confront the full spectrum of past injustices, including those perpetrated by our own ancestors. To move forward ethically, we must address all facets of our history with equal scrutiny and empathy.

The San people, traditionally a nomadic hunter-gatherer group, freely roamed the plains of Southern Africa, living off the land and moving with the seasons. The Khoi people, herders with livestock, entered Southern Africa and began to integrate with the San. This integration led to the formation of communities with clans, chiefs, and defined territories. Later, the Bantu Xhosa people also arrived in the region. Initially, there were conflicts between these groups, but over time, they managed to achieve a level of integration. This historical scenario prompts an intriguing question: what if these groups had fully integrated into a single nation? What would have happened when the Dutch arrived if the San, Khoi, and Xhosa had discarded their distinct clans, languages, and beliefs to form one strong, unified nation? A fully integrated nation might have presented a formidable front against the Dutch colonizers. The combined strengths and resources of the San, Khoi, and Xhosa could have resulted in a more robust defence. The San's deep knowledge of the land, the Khoi's livestock and herding skills, and the Xhosa's agricultural and military prowess would have created a well-rounded and resilient society. Such unity might have deterred Dutch advances or at least prolonged resistance, potentially altering the course of colonial encounters in Southern Africa. Moreover, a unified nation would have fostered a sense of collective identity and purpose, transcending individual tribal affiliations. This union could have led to the development of a common language, culture, and set of beliefs, enhancing internal cohesion and stability. The political and social structures would likely have been stronger, providing better organization and strategic planning in the face of external threats. The proposed unified nation of the San, Khoi, and Xhosa poses a significant counterfactual to history. While it is impossible to predict with certainty what the exact outcomes would have been, it is reasonable to speculate that such a nation would have been better positioned to resist colonization. The historical route of Southern Africa might have been distinctly different, with profound implications for the region's development, identity, and legacy.

The Khoisan experience offers profound lessons on resilience, adaptation, and the complexities of cultural pride in the face of external pressures. The Xhosa proverb, "the gospel gets bitten into the head of an unbeliever," highlights the harsh reality that resistance to change can lead to dire consequences. For the Khoisan, their steadfast adherence to their traditional ways in a rapidly changing world may have been both their strength and their downfall. One significant aspect that cost the Khoisan dearly was their deep pride in their identity and their reluctance to adapt to the encroaching influences. Their determination to maintain their nomadic, hunter-gatherer lifestyle and cultural practices, while admirable, left them vulnerable to the expansionist ambitions of both Bantu tribes and European colonizers. In a world that was increasingly moving towards settled agriculture and centralized political structures, the Khoisan's resistance to change rendered them less capable of defending their territories and way of life. However, the question arises, should the Khoisan have shed their traditional ways and beliefs to adapt to the changing world? While adaptation is a natural survival strategy, the loss of cultural identity and heritage is a significant cost. The possibility of uniting with neighbouring clans and Bantu tribes to form a larger, stronger nation could have provided a strategic advantage against external threats. Unity would have pooled resources, knowledge, and strength, potentially creating a more resilient and cohesive society. The broader implication for contemporary Africa is the exploration of unity as a form of salvation. The idea of unifying the continent, or at least fostering stronger alliances among African nations, resonates with the vision of Pan Africanism. Unity could address common challenges, such as economic instability, political fragmentation, and external exploitation. By coming together, African nations could leverage their collective strengths, share resources, and create a more powerful and influential presence on the global stage.

Some noble ideas are commendable and often excel in theoretical contexts but falter in practical application. Such is the case with this ideology; we are inherently incapable of uniting and achieving consensus. Historical evidence underscores this powerlessness; during the peak of the transatlantic slave trade, the lucrative nature of slavery was enabled by clans and tribes who were quick to capture and sell their rivals into bondage. This willingness to exploit others for personal gain illustrates the deep-seated divisions and self-serving interests that undermine collective unity, revealing the harsh reality that some idealistic visions may remain unattainable in practice.

2

fool

The term "fool" as a verb is defined as to trick or deceive. Individuals of African descent who dedicate their lives to Pan-Africanism and the vision of uniting the continent cannot be labelled as fools; rather, they have been trapped by the allure of this Pan-Africanist dream. It is a touching realisation that many ideologies, including Pan-Africanism, often find their origins outside the African continent. Yet, rather than creating indigenous ideologies, there is a tendency to adopt foreign concepts such as Communism, Socialism, and feminism, attempting to redefine and defend these imported ideologies as our own. This phenomenon reflects a broader pattern of embracing foreign ideologies without critically evaluating their relevance and applicability within the African context. The challenge lies in the need to cultivate a culture of introspection and innovation, fostering the development of authentically African ideologies that are rooted in the continent's diverse histories, cultures, and experiences. Only through this process of redefinition and creation can Africans move beyond the confines of borrowed ideologies and shape a future that is truly reflective of their unique perspectives and aspirations.

The book examines the perspectives of Pan-Africanists who advocate for a borderless Africa, envisioning the continent as a unified "United States of Africa" or a singular country. This viewpoint is subjected to scrutiny within the book's analysis. The argument suggested is that the notion of a borderless Africa, parallel to a unified nation state, oversimplifies the complexities inherent in the continent's diverse cultures, histories, and geopolitical realities. Proponents of this ideology often emphasize the eradication of colonial imposed borders, viewing them as barriers to true African unity. However, the book challenges this perspective by highlighting the intricate web of ethnicities, languages, and historical narratives that define Africa's multifaceted identity. It contends that the imposition of a single, homogenous African nation overlooks the nuanced dynamics of local identities and governance structures that have evolved over centuries. Moreover, the practicality and feasibility of transitioning to a unified continental entity, considering the existing political and economic disparities among African nations, are subjects of critical inquiry. By engaging with these complexities, the book aims to foster a nuanced understanding of Pan-Africanism, advocating for a discourse that acknowledges the importance of unity while recognizing the diverse and evolving nature of Africa's socio-political landscape. For a span of 13 years, I ardently adhered to Marxist communism, embracing its ideology, and sincerely believing myself to be a communist. During this time, I fervently advocated for communism as the definitive solution for Africa's challenges. Despite persistent challenges from friends who pointed out discrepancies in my adherence to communist principles, I staunchly defended my position with various rationales. I argued that my pursuit of personal wealth did not contradict my commitment to a classless society, emphasizing that I did not possess ownership of the means of production. However, a pivotal realization dawned upon me: I discovered that my professed beliefs did not align with my actions and attitudes. Despite my affirmed commitment to communism, I unconsciously upheld a class system in my personal interactions and preferences. There existed a particular class of individuals with whom I harboured reservations about sharing spaces, a revelation that starkly contradicted my professed ideals of equality and classlessness. Given this introspective journey, I refrain from providing a definitive definition of Pan-Africanism. Instead, I recognize the complexities and nuances within ideologies, acknowledging the multifaceted nature of Pan-Africanist thought. My personal evolution serves as a cautionary tale, underscoring the importance of critically examining one's beliefs and actions to ensure alignment with the principles one advocates. Through this introspection, I advocate for a enlightened understanding of Pan-Africanism that embraces its diversity of perspectives and challenges simplistic definitions. In this work, I refrain from delving into the origins and evolution of Pan-Africanism due to its ongoing and dynamic nature. Africans commonly embrace foreign ideologies across various spheres such as politics, finance, and religion. When encountering shortcomings in these foreign concepts, rather than acknowledging their ineffectiveness, there is a tendency to rationalize them. Consequently, individuals may delve into historical archives, seeking connections that are not inherently present.

Regardless of the accuracy of any presented argument, Africans often find ways to justify their perspectives. This propensity leads me to omit discussions on the historical backdrop and key figures in Pan-Africanism. Generally, Pan-Africanism rests on three pillars: African Nationalism, Socialism, and continental unity. Personally, I align with the latter pillar, however, the realization of this aspiration appears elusive.

3

the impact of the Willie Lynch myth and daddy issues

In 1712, at James River in Virginia, William Lynch delivered a notorious speech to American slave owners. Lynch, a plantation owner from the British West Indies, purportedly outlined a method for controlling slaves without resorting to physical violence. His strategy, as recounted, emphasized setting slaves against each other, utilizing Colourism as a potent tool, and establishing a class system among them. This speech, later transcribed into a letter titled 'The Making of a Slave,' has been widely debunked as a myth or hoax. However, the veracity of its origins does not negate the recognition of a strategic method devised to control oppressed people, particularly Africans, through systematic conditioning. Throughout history, various myths have shaped societies profoundly, such as the impactful story of Jesus Christ, despite the lack of conclusive evidence of his existence. The relevance of the Willie Lynch narrative lies in its reflection of a broader pattern: the tendency of marginalized communities to externalize blame for their challenges. Africans often attribute their social ills to the legacies of apartheid, colonization, and mental conditioning. While it is true that years of oppression have mentally conditioned black individuals to turn against one another, it is equally valid to argue against a simplistic view of humans as easily tamed creatures capable of swift behavioural changes. The core of this argument lies in the responsibility for change. Rather than solely blaming external historical forces, there is a call for introspection and acknowledgment of internal dynamics. Ghana's attainment of independence in 1957 marked a significant milestone, positioning it as one of the earliest African nations to break free from colonial rule. Conversely, South Africa's journey to independence was long-drawn-out, with its formal independence granted much later. Despite this conflict in timelines, both countries share a common narrative of grappling with the legacies of colonialism and apartheid respectively. Reflecting on South Africa's post-apartheid era, which commenced in 1994, the nation has had over three decades to navigate its path toward progress and societal transformation. However, a persistent phenomenon emerges: the tendency to attribute current challenges to the enduring effects of apartheid. This narrative often serves as a convenient explanation for shortcomings and failures, deflecting responsibility from the choices and actions taken since gaining independence. Indeed, the enduring legacy of apartheid cannot be understated, particularly its profound impact on social structures, economic disparities, and the psychological fabric of the nation. Yet, the question arises; How do independent states, armed with freedom and governance, grapple with the inability to effect substantial changes for the betterment of their societies? The rhetoric of blaming apartheid for all ills can become a barrier to progress, stifling the urgency for proactive, homegrown solutions. Independent nations possess the power and agency to enact policies, implement reforms, and foster inclusive development. However, the narrative of historical conditioning often eclipses the need for bold, innovative approaches to tackle contemporary challenges.

To move forward, a shift in mindset is imperative. Acknowledging the impact of the past while embracing agency in the present is a delicate balance. It requires leadership that inspires accountability, citizens who actively participate in shaping their futures, and a collective will to break free from the constraints of historical narratives. Only through such introspection and action can nations like South Africa chart a course toward genuine progress and a future unburdened by the shadows of the past. The contention that African states lack true autonomy and freedom often surfaces in discussions about the continent's challenges. Yet, this very argument underscores a deeper issue: the persistent fragmentation and disunity within Africa. The notion of African unity remains elusive, overshadowed by a prevailing lack of loyalty and pervasive jealousy among its peoples. The attainment of independence by African nations was not a passive reception of freedom; rather, it was the product of negotiations and compromises. These newly independent states willingly assumed debts from international institutions such as the International Monetary Fund (IMF) and the World Bank, making choices that would impact their economic trajectories. However, the subsequent trajectory of many African nations points to a different narrative, one marred by internal conflicts, corruption, and mismanagement. Blaming external forces for Africa's struggles becomes a limited perspective when considering the internal dynamics at play. It is Africans themselves who engage in acts of violence, betrayal, and the exploitation of national resources for personal gain. The perpetuation of poverty among African populations is not solely due to historical legacies or external interference but is often worsened by internal actions and decisions. This introspection raises uncomfortable truths about the state of African governance and leadership. The lack of loyalty and the prevalence of jealousy among Africans hinder efforts toward unity and progress. The disunity that persists among African nations, manifested in conflicts and rivalries, undermines the potential for collective growth and development. The prevailing issue plaguing the African continent resides in its repeated reliance on external players to address internal challenges. This recurring pattern reflects a deeply ingrained "daddy complex" wherein Africa habitually seeks overprotective guidance and support from foreign powers. Historically, this dependency complex was exemplified by the continent's divided allegiance during the Cold War era, when it sought assistance from global superpowers such as the United States of America and the Soviet Union. Despite purported strides towards self-determination, exemplified by participation in organizations like BRICS (Brazil, Russia, India, China, and South Africa), Africa's underlying dependence remains steadfast. While allegedly aiming for mutual benefit, the reality often entails African nations assuming inferior roles, serving as mere pawns in a geopolitical chess game orchestrated by more powerful players. Notably, emerging powers such as China and Russia have strategically positioned themselves to capitalize on Africa's vulnerabilities and resources.

China has ascended as Africa's new patron, leveraging its economic prowess to forge strategic partnerships with African nations. However, this relationship is characterized by uneven power dynamics, with China wielding considerable influence while trapping African countries in a web of debt diplomacy. As China expands its footprint across the continent, ostensibly for economic development, concerns mount over the exploitation and plundering of Africa's natural resources. The perpetuation of this "daddy complex" perpetuates a cycle of dependency and suppression, undermining Africa's autonomy and inhibiting its ability to chart an independent path towards development and prosperity. To break free from this paradigm, African nations must prioritize self-reliance, foster intracontinental cooperation, and assertively negotiate equitable partnerships with external actors. Only through genuine agency and autonomy can Africa transcend its legacy of dependency and emerge as a formidable player on the global stage. Continuously attributing Africa's challenges to the legacies of colonialism, slavery, and apartheid represents a tacit acceptance of inferiority and a surrender to deterministic narratives. Such an approach suggests a resignation to the belief that Africans are akin to programmable entities, devoid of agency or the capacity for self-determination. By perpetually casting blame on historical injustices, Africa risks perpetuating a narrative of victimhood and dependency, wherein external forces dictate the course of its development. This paradigm equates to relinquishing the role of protagonist in shaping Africa's destiny, relegating its inhabitants to passive passengers rather than active agents in charting their own trajectories. The metaphorical imagery of being "staff on the boat of life" underscores a sense of powerlessness and subservience, wherein Africans are relegated to subordinate roles within a predetermined narrative. Instead of assuming the mantle of leadership and steering their own destinies, Africans are depicted as mere bystanders, subject to the whims of historical forces beyond their control. The implication of this narrative extends beyond a mere acknowledgement of past injustices; it perpetuates a cycle of dependency and disempowerment. By framing Africa's present challenges solely within the context of its colonial past, the continent risks abandoning responsibility for its own future. This narrative constrains Africa within a deterministic basis, wherein progress is contingent upon the benevolence of external actors or the rectification of historical wrongs.

To transcend this model, Africa must reject the narrative of victimhood and reclaim agency over its own destiny. This entails acknowledging the enduring legacy of colonialism and slavery while simultaneously asserting agency and autonomy in shaping a future defined by self-determination and empowerment. Only by assuming the role of captains of their own destinies can Africans break free from the shackles of history and chart a course towards a brighter, more prosperous future. To truly move forward, Africa must confront these internal challenges with a sense of responsibility and accountability. It requires leaders who prioritize the common good over personal gain, citizens committed to the welfare of their nations, and a shift away from the culture of betrayal and self-interest. Only through such fundamental changes can Africa begin to harness its vast resources for the benefit of all its people, paving the way for genuine unity and progress.

4

Berlin Hangover

The Berlin Conference of 1884/85, conversationally termed the 'Scramble for Africa,' is frequently cited as a pivotal event in shaping Africa's contemporary geopolitical landscape. At this conference, European powers convened to partition and demarcate territorial boundaries across the African continent, often disregarding pre-existing ethnic, cultural, and religious affiliations. This random allocation of borders has been implicated as a primary factor contributing to the conflicts and tensions that have plagued Africa in subsequent years. The allocation of territories at the Berlin Conference often resulted in the consolidation of different ethnic groups, clans, and tribes within the confines of newly drawn borders. This imposed cohabitation of culturally distinct communities without their input or consent laid the groundwork for internal discord and intercommunal conflicts. The forced amalgamation of diverse populations, often with conflicting interests and identities, sowed seeds of discord that continue to echo throughout the continent. Indeed, the aftermath of the Berlin Conference has been marked by recurrent episodes of ethnic and tribal strife, fuelled by grievances rooted in historical injustices and territorial disputes. The subtext underlying many of Africa's conflicts is the quest for autonomy and self-determination among distinct ethnic groups and communities. However, it is essential to recognize that while the legacy of the Berlin Conference looms large in Africa's history, it is not the sole determinant of the continent's conflicts. The difficulties of African conflicts are multifaceted, encompassing a myriad of socio-economic, political, and historical factors. While the random division of territories undoubtedly worsened tensions, the underlying causes of conflict often extend beyond mere territorial demarcations. In essence, while acknowledging the role of the Berlin Conference in shaping Africa's present-day challenges, it is crucial to adopt a nuanced understanding of the continent's conflicts. Addressing these conflicts needs comprehensive strategies that address the root causes of discord while fostering inclusivity, dialogue, and respect for diverse cultural identities and aspirations. The Berlin Conference resolutions, while historically significant, are not binding declarations carved in stone. The notion that Africans are beholden to these colonial-era divisions is both fallacious and defeatist. There exists a tangible opportunity for Africans to assert agency and reclaim control over the destiny of their continent. What delays progress is not the lack of agency but rather the absence of collective will and leadership. The suggestion of convening a new, inclusive conference to redefine Africa's boundaries and reshape its geopolitical landscape is not only viable but imperative. Such a conference, founded on principles of inclusivity and sovereignty, presents a platform for African nations to assert their autonomy and reshape their destinies. The persistent recourse to blaming the Berlin Conference serves as a convenient scapegoat, deflecting attention from the failure of African leaders to chart a course towards unity and progress. If the mere amalgamation of tribes and nations under colonial rule precipitates conflict, the prospect of uniting an entire continent may seem daunting. However, it is precisely in the face of such challenges that bold and visionary leadership is required. The reluctance to embark on such a transformative endeavour betrays a lack of ambition and courage among African leaders. It is high time for Africans to reject the shackles of colonialism and forge a new path forward. Through unity, determination, and a steadfast commitment to self-determination, Africans can transcend the legacy of division and chart a course towards a brighter, more prosperous future. The blame game must cease, and action must be taken to reclaim Africa's rightful place on the global stage.

5

Tribal Hangover

Throughout my life, I have maintained a profound sense of pride in my surname and ancestral heritage as a member of the Hlubi tribe. Distinct from the Zulu and Xhosa ethnic groups, I have consistently endeavoured to elucidate my cultural identity to others. Central to this explanation is the assertion that my lineage traces its origins to the KwaZulu region, distinct from the Zulu heartland. Amidst Shaka's consolidation of power and formation of the Zulu Kingdom through conquest, the Hlubi remained unsoiled, retaining their distinct identity. The distinction between the Hlubi and neighbouring ethnicities, particularly the Xhosa, often necessitates elaborate clarification. While some may erroneously categorize me as Xhosa, I diligently underscore the historical trajectory of the Hlubi migration to the Eastern Cape. This migration was not voluntary but rather a response to conflicts with English colonial forces. Consequently, my people sought refuge in the Eastern Cape, where they encountered a landscape fraught with socio-political complexities, including discrimination from the Xhosa population. Navigating these intricacies of identity becomes a recurring endeavour, requiring meticulous explanation to dispel misconceptions and affirm my cultural heritage. Emphasizing the unique historical experiences of the Hlubi, including their resilience in the face of external pressures and migrations, becomes imperative in delineating the boundaries of my identity. Despite the challenges posed by misperceptions and historical complexities, I steadfastly uphold my allegiance to the Hlubi tribe, perpetuating a legacy of resilience and cultural pride amidst an ever-evolving social landscape.

As I mature, my perspective on the significance of pride in my history and identity undergoes a transformation. While acknowledging the importance of understanding and preserving our collective heritage, I increasingly question the tangible benefits that such pride brings to Africans. Although our history holds immense value in shaping our identities, the emphasis on cultural pride, clan affiliations, and tribalism can inadvertently contribute to societal divisions and hinder progress. Clarity becomes evident that the celebration of cultural distinctions often exacerbates social fragmentation. Tribal loyalties and historical grievances perpetuate intergroup tensions, impeding national unity and socioeconomic development. Rather than fostering cohesion, the emphasis on cultural pride can inadvertently reinforce divisive narratives, hindering collective advancement. Considering these reflections, I propose a re-evaluation of the role of historical pride in contemporary African society. While advocating for the preservation of our rich cultural heritage through museums, historical texts, and academic research, I contend that the active promotion of tribal affiliations and clan loyalties may be counterproductive in the pursuit of national unity and progress. Instead, efforts should be directed towards fostering a sense of pan-African identity grounded in shared values and aspirations, transcending the boundaries of ethnicity and lineage. By relegating the emphasis on tribalism and clan allegiance to the realm of historical documentation, African societies can prioritize collective solidarity and inclusive nation-building. This does not diminish the significance of our diverse cultural traditions but rather emphasises forward-looking approach that prioritizes unity and progress. Ultimately, the preservation of our history remains paramount, but its relevance in shaping contemporary identities must be critically examined to navigate towards a more cohesive and prosperous future for Africa.

6

GIMME GIMME GIMME MORE

Corruption is an intrinsic aspect of human nature, and when coupled with power, its manifestations become even more pronounced. The saying "power corrupts" encapsulates this phenomenon, highlighting how authority and influence can exacerbate corrupt behaviours. Instances of everyday corruption are pervasive and often go unnoticed, yet they illustrate the extent to which individuals are willing to exploit personal connections and power dynamics for personal gain. Consider the scenario of visiting a bank with an extensive queue. If a person has a friend who works at the bank and uses this relationship to bypass the queue, this act is a subtle yet clear example of corruption. Likewise, in social settings such as clubs, where long queues are common, leveraging a friendship with a bouncer to gain expedited entry through non-traditional routes, such as the kitchen, further exemplifies how personal connections can facilitate corrupt practices. Moreover, interactions with law enforcement often reveal another layer of everyday corruption. For instance, when a traffic violation occurs, the temptation to offer a bribe to a traffic officer to avoid a fine is a widespread practice. This not only undermines the legal system but also perpetuates a cycle of corruption that erodes trust in public institutions.

These examples underscore the ubiquitous nature of corruption, demonstrating how it permeates various aspects of daily life. The propensity for individuals to engage in corrupt acts when opportunities arise, particularly when power or influence is involved, suggests that corruption is not merely a systemic issue but a deeply ingrained human behaviour. Addressing this requires a comprehensive understanding of the psychological and social factors that drive corruption, as well as robust systems of accountability to mitigate its impact. Recognizing and confronting the everyday manifestations of corruption is crucial in fostering a culture of integrity and ethical behaviour.

Corruption is not exclusive to Africa; it is a pervasive international problem affecting various regions worldwide. However, a critical distinction lies in how corruption impacts citizens differently across regions. In the Global West, although corruption exists, it often does not significantly detract from the entitlements and services that citizens receive. The systems in place typically ensure that, despite instances of corruption, the fundamental rights and benefits due to the populace are maintained. Power inherently involves the ability to influence and make preferential decisions, often benefiting associates and allies. This aspect of power dynamics is universal and can be observed in both personal and professional spheres globally. Nevertheless, the crucial factor that differentiates the impact of corruption in different contexts is the balance within the system. Effective governance requires that, despite the potential for corrupt practices, the overarching system remains equitable and prioritizes the well-being of citizens. In political spheres, it is imperative that those in positions of power and influence prioritize the needs and interests of the populace. Ensuring that citizens' rights and benefits are safeguarded should be the foremost responsibility of any government or leadership. A balanced system of governance involves mechanisms of accountability and transparency that mitigate the adverse effects of corruption and ensure that public resources and services are allocated fairly and efficiently. Therefore, addressing corruption requires more than merely acknowledging its existence; it demands the implementation of robust structures that prioritize citizen welfare above individual or collective corrupt interests. Establishing such a system is crucial for fostering trust in public institutions and ensuring that the rights and entitlements of citizens are upheld regardless of the underlying power dynamics. Recognizing and actively combating the disparities in how corruption affects different regions is essential for promoting global equity and justice.

What frustrates me deeply is the prevailing discourse that predominantly focuses on global influences keeping Africa disadvantaged and historical injustices. While these issues are undeniably significant, they often overshadow the critical problem of corruption that plagues the continent. Corruption remains a pervasive and destructive force, undermining the potential for development and equitable resource distribution. The absence of stringent punishment for corrupt practices exacerbates this issue, allowing those in power to exploit public resources without accountability. Despite Africa's wealth of resources, these assets seldom benefit the general populace. Instead, they are misappropriated by a corrupt elite, leaving most citizens deprived of essential services and opportunities. This misallocation of resources perpetuates poverty and stifles economic growth, hindering the continent's progress. One of the unique challenges in Africa is the way voters make electoral decisions. Emotional and historical contexts heavily influence voting patterns, often at the expense of rational assessment of candidates' integrity and competence. This tendency to vote based on sentiment rather than scrutinizing candidates' records on corruption perpetuates a cycle of ineffective governance and mismanagement. Furthermore, there is a pervasive reluctance among the populace to hold corrupt leaders accountable. Instead of confronting corruption directly, there is a tendency to attribute Africa's challenges to external factors and historical injustices. While these factors are undeniably relevant, using them as an excuse for inaction against corruption undermines efforts to address the root causes of the continent's stagnation.

For Africa to move forward, it is imperative that corruption is confronted head-on, with robust systems of accountability and transparent governance. The electorate must prioritize integrity and competence over emotional and historical affiliations, demanding better governance and equitable resource distribution. Only through such collective efforts can Africa transcend its current challenges and unlock its full potential.

7

Blaconomics

In the heart of Atteridgeville, a vibrant township, I was actively involved in an internet café that offered a range of services. Our establishment provided design services, T-shirt printing, promotional material printing, internet access, and CV typing for residents. My specific role in the business was to offer business solutions, including writing business plans and company profiles for small and medium-sized enterprises, as well as preparing tender documents for entrepreneurs. Through our extensive database of CVs, I had access to a substantial sample pool, allowing me to analyse the socioeconomic conditions of the working-class population. Engaging in conversations with our clients further deepened my understanding of their challenges and aspirations. This experience led to a sobering realization: one cannot save the world alone, and despite leading a horse to water, it cannot be compelled to drink. A prevalent mindset among many of our clients was to perform only the bare minimum required. For individuals from rural areas, possessing basic computer literacy, particularly knowledge of Microsoft Word, was often perceived as a significant achievement, equating to a special qualification. However, this limited skill set did not align with the broader demands of the modern job market. This disparity highlights a critical issue in addressing poverty and underemployment. While access to technology and basic skills training is essential, it is not sufficient on its own. There needs to be a broader emphasis on comprehensive education and skills development that goes beyond minimal proficiency. Encouraging a mindset of continuous learning and adaptation is crucial for fostering real economic empowerment and upward mobility. Ultimately, my experience at the internet café underscored the importance of addressing both the structural and attitudinal barriers that hinder progress. Providing tools and opportunities is only part of the solution; fostering a culture of ambition and resilience is equally vital in driving meaningful change in underserved communities. Many of my clients sought my assistance, frequently inquiring about the way forward and consistently requesting discounts on my services. This pattern was prevalent among various demographics, but particularly notable among the black middle class. These individuals, often residing in suburban areas, would travel to the township to avail themselves of our services when they found the prices of white-owned businesses prohibitive. This behaviour highlights a troubling dynamic wherein black middle-class clients exploit black-owned businesses in the township. They are aware that the quality of work offered is on par with that of white-owned enterprises, yet they seek to benefit from lower prices. This practice not only undermines the value of black businesses but also perpetuates a cycle of economic disparity within the community. The expectation for discounted services reveals underlying issues of economic inequality and systemic exploitation. While seeking affordability is understandable, the tendency to devalue black-owned services in favour of cost savings reflects a deeper lack of support and solidarity within the black community. This dynamic can be detrimental to the growth and sustainability of black businesses, which are crucial for fostering economic empowerment and resilience in marginalized areas. Furthermore, the repeated requests for discounts also underscore the financial constraints faced by many clients, even within the middle class. This indicates a broader issue of economic instability and the challenges of maintaining financial security in a system that often marginalizes black communities. To address these issues, it is essential to promote fair pricing practices that reflect the true value of black-owned services while encouraging the community to support and invest in its own businesses. Strengthening economic solidarity within the black community can help break the cycle of exploitation and contribute to the overall economic upliftment of the township and beyond.

Over the years, I have embarked on numerous entrepreneurial ventures, all of which ultimately failed. I produced vape juices, launched a high-quality clothing brand capable of competing globally, organized social markets, and hosted events. Despite my efforts and dedication to quality and service, none of these businesses succeeded. The feedback I received was disheartening: my businesses failed because the target market did not prioritize quality or service. Instead, success was heavily influenced by the persona behind the venture. I was advised that to succeed, I needed to involve a well-known thug or an attractive individual who could draw public interest.

This insight was particularly revealing. It highlighted a pervasive attitude within the community that places more value on the identity of the business owner than on the quality of the product or service offered. My business solutions enterprise thrived because it was unique in the services it provided, and I had no competitors. However, this experience taught me that support from the black community is contingent upon two critical factors: the identity of the business initiator and the maintenance of a working-class appearance. One of the most significant lessons I learned is the importance of not displaying signs of wealth accrued from their support. There exists a "crabs in a bucket" mentality where visible success can lead to a withdrawal of support. The origins of this mentality, while rooted in historical oppression, are less important than addressing its current impact. It is crucial to recognize that many nations have experienced oppression yet have managed to rise above it through perseverance and unity. For the black community to foster genuine economic growth and entrepreneurial success, it is essential to transcend these limiting mentalities and prioritize merit, quality, and collective advancement. Africans and black people globally exhibit a unique reluctance to support their own businesses. As soon as a black entrepreneur attains financial success, there is a swift inclination to patronize famous international brands, notably Italian ones, thereby diverting economic resources away from their own community. This phenomenon is not confined to one region but is observed worldwide. Black-owned businesses, despite their quality and potential, often struggle due to a lack of sustained support from their community. Prominent examples of this trend include brands like 'Stoned Cherrie', 'Sun Goddess', and 'FUBU'. These brands initially garnered significant support from the black community but eventually faced decline as their founders' success became apparent. The support dwindles as black consumers perceive that their patronage is enriching someone within their own race, leading to a withdrawal of support. This pattern suggests a deeper, systemic issue where economic solidarity within the black community is undermined by a preference for external validation and status symbols associated with non-black brands. The impact is detrimental to the growth and sustainability of black-owned businesses, which are essential for fostering economic empowerment and self-sufficiency within the community. Addressing this issue requires a cultural shift towards valuing and prioritizing black-owned enterprises. It involves recognizing the importance of circulating wealth within the community to build robust economic foundations. Furthermore, it is crucial to dismantle the psychological barriers that perpetuate this cycle of disinvestment in black businesses. By fostering a sense of pride and responsibility in supporting black entrepreneurs, the community can break free from this limiting mindset. Emphasizing the quality and value of black-owned products and services, and celebrating their success as a collective achievement, can pave the way for a more prosperous and self-reliant black economy. The challenges facing black economics present a double-edged sword, with responsibility lying on both business owners and consumers. On the one hand, many emerging black businesses often lack fundamental business principles. These include providing high-quality service, maintaining professionalism, adhering to time commitments, and fulfilling promises made to clients. Such shortcomings can significantly undermine the credibility and sustainability of these businesses, leading to customer dissatisfaction and a tarnished reputation. On the other hand, black consumers frequently seek discounts and are unwilling to pay premium prices for products and services from black-owned businesses. This behaviour overlooks the broader importance of supporting these businesses for the economic upliftment of the community. Unlike established businesses, emerging black businesses typically lack the purchasing power to buy in bulk or negotiate favourable pricing, which often results in higher costs for their goods and services. Consumers' reluctance to pay these prices further exacerbates the financial challenges these businesses face, making it difficult for them to achieve economies of scale and competitive pricing. This dynamic creates a vicious cycle where black businesses struggle to grow and improve due to insufficient revenue and investment. Without consistent support from their community, they are unable to build the necessary infrastructure, expand their operations, or improve their service quality. Consequently, they remain at a disadvantage compared to larger, more established enterprises. To break this cycle, it is crucial for black consumers to understand and appreciate the long-term benefits of supporting black-owned businesses. This support is not merely about transactions but about building a resilient economic foundation within the community. Simultaneously, black entrepreneurs must strive to enhance their business practices, emphasizing quality, reliability, and customer satisfaction. Bridging this gap requires a concerted effort from both sides to foster a culture of mutual support and excellence, ultimately leading to a thriving black economy.

How can a people who struggle to support one another expect to unite communities, nations, and a continent? This paradox highlights a profound issue within the African context, where the inability to foster mutual support undermines broader aspirations for unity and collective progress. The persistence of the Willie Lynch myth mentality, which perpetuates division and distrust among black individuals, continues to hinder efforts toward genuine cohesion and solidarity. What exacerbates this frustration is the existence of leaders on this continent who genuinely care about the well-being of their people. Their efforts are often stymied by systemic issues and the pervasive mentality that prioritizes individual success over collective advancement. More disheartening is the role of academics, who, despite their intellectual prowess, remain preoccupied with historical analyses of our current predicament. While understanding the past is crucial, an overemphasis on historical grievances without actionable steps towards improvement becomes counterproductive. Significant research has been conducted to understand the historical and structural factors contributing to Africa's current challenges. The time has come to pivot from merely diagnosing problems to implementing solutions. The focus must shift to developing practical strategies that address the root causes of disunity and economic stagnation. This includes fostering a culture of support within the community, promoting entrepreneurial growth, and implementing policies that encourage collaboration and mutual benefit.

Moreover, African academics and intellectuals must leverage their knowledge to propose innovative solutions and influence policymaking. By prioritizing actionable insights and pragmatic approaches, they can contribute to building a resilient and united continent. It is imperative to move beyond historical lamentation and channel our collective energies towards creating a future where African communities and nations can thrive together. This requires a concerted effort to cultivate a mindset of solidarity, accountability, and proactive problem-solving, ultimately leading to a more united and prosperous Africa.

8

Family structure

Art imitates life, and life imitates art. This interplay is particularly significant when considering the influence of art and entertainment as tools for propaganda. Unlike other communities, black people are often depicted through social media and media platforms in a manner that accentuates their negative shortcomings. Art, a powerful medium for conveying messages and shaping perceptions, can be weaponized to push specific agendas and manipulate how individuals see themselves and others. In many instances, the portrayal of black individuals in art and media is skewed towards emphasizing stereotypes and reinforcing negative perceptions. This manipulation extends beyond mere representation; it shapes societal attitudes and perpetuates systemic biases. By consistently highlighting deficiencies or negative attributes, media can influence public opinion and foster a sense of inferiority within the black community. This strategic use of art and entertainment to propagate certain narratives underscores the significant impact media has on societal norms and individual self-perception. Moreover, art and media are potent tools for setting agendas and guiding public discourse. When used responsibly, they can inspire and uplift communities, fostering unity and progress. However, when misused, they become instruments of division and manipulation. The deliberate portrayal of black individuals in a negative light serves to reinforce prejudices and maintain social hierarchies. This manipulation is not always overt; it can be subtle, shaping subconscious biases and influencing behaviour in ways that are difficult to detect. The challenge lies in recognizing and countering these manipulative tactics. It is essential to promote diverse and accurate representations of black individuals in art and media, highlighting their strengths, achievements, and contributions. By doing so, it is possible to counteract the negative narratives and foster a more inclusive and equitable society. Empowering black artists and creators to tell their own stories and control their narratives is a critical step towards achieving this goal. Through conscious effort and advocacy, art and media can be reclaimed as tools for positive change and community empowerment.

In contrast to historical trends where media executives were predominantly white, there has been a significant shift, particularly in Africa. Despite this progress, black creatives continue to produce content that perpetuates negative stereotypes about black people. Negative portrayals are especially prevalent in representations of relationships. Positive depictions of black love and relationships are conspicuously absent in both music and cinema. Similarly, the portrayal of loving black family structures remains scarce. This persistent focus on negative imagery undermines the diversity and richness of black experiences, contributing to a skewed and often detrimental perception of black communities.

Growing up in the 1990s, the music, movies, and television series of that era profoundly shaped my worldview and that of my peers. As teenagers, our primary mission in life was to find true love, a quest that was deeply embedded in our collective consciousness. We believed in the ideal of love and sought to understand and embody its core values. This included connecting with someone on a profound level and finding a partner who would prioritize us in their lives. Our aspiration for true love was not merely a fleeting teenage infatuation but a deeply rooted desire, significantly influenced by the cultural content we consumed. The media of the 90s frequently portrayed romantic relationships as central to personal fulfilment and happiness. Music lyrics celebrated the pursuit and experience of love, while movies and television series often revolved around romantic plots, emphasizing the importance of finding a soulmate. These portrayals instilled in us the belief that love was not only attainable but essential for a fulfilling life. Our primary goal in life extended beyond just finding love; it encompassed the broader vision of getting married and building a beautiful family. We were inherently family-oriented, valuing the concept of a loving, supportive family unit as the cornerstone of a happy and successful life. The narratives we absorbed from media reinforced the notion that a harmonious family was the ultimate achievement, shaping our aspirations and guiding our life choices. In essence, the cultural milieu of the 1990s played a pivotal role in moulding our values and aspirations. The emphasis on love and family in the music, movies, and television series of that era instilled in us a deep-seated belief in the importance of these ideals, guiding our journey towards forming meaningful and lasting relationships.

The reason for my preceding statement lies in addressing the critical issue facing Africa today: the erosion of family structure. The relentless pursuit of material wealth has eclipsed the traditional focus on maintaining strong family units. For Africa to truly prosper, it is essential to reestablish and prioritize robust family values and structures. A continent, nation, or community lacking these foundational elements is inevitably destined for hardship. The weakening of family bonds has far-reaching consequences, contributing significantly to many of the social ills prevalent in African societies. Issues such as crime, poverty, and social instability can often be traced back to the neglect of family structures and values. The abandonment of these principles, which once provided stability and guidance, has left a void that materialism alone cannot fill. The shift in societal values from character-based judgments to financial assessments further exacerbates this problem. Men are increasingly judged by their financial status rather than their integrity, moral character, and ability to contribute positively to their families and communities. Strong family units are vital for the social and economic well-being of a society. They provide emotional support, instil values, and foster environments where individuals can thrive. In the absence of such structures, communities suffer from a lack of cohesion and direction. Children are adversely affected, growing up without the necessary guidance and support that strong family units traditionally provide. This lack of a stable familial foundation often leads to cycles of poverty and social dysfunction, perpetuating the very issues that hinder Africa's progress. Reestablishing a focus on family values and structures is imperative for Africa's future. By emphasizing love, respect, and character over material wealth, African societies can rebuild the strong family units that are essential for enduring prosperity and stability. Addressing this fundamental issue is crucial for overcoming the myriad challenges facing the continent today.

Art, in its various forms, should indeed draw inspiration from real life, reflecting the complexities and nuances of human experiences. However, there is a discernible difference in how different racial groups are portrayed in media, particularly in music and cinema. White people, for example, have a longstanding tradition of curating their image through media to emphasize moral integrity and stable relationships. Even when infidelity is depicted in white genres, it is often framed as an anomaly—a deviation from their moral code that requires rectification. This controlled narrative fosters a perception of white individuals as inherently virtuous and morally upright. In stark contrast, black genres of music, film, and social media frequently depict black people in a more negative light, emphasizing promiscuity and a preoccupation with sex. These portrayals suggest that black individuals are more inclined to engage in infidelity and transactional sexual relationships. Such representations can perpetuate harmful stereotypes, influencing public perception and reinforcing societal biases. The disparity in these portrayals is not a reflection of inherent differences between racial groups but rather a consequence of the power dynamics within media production and the narratives that are chosen to be amplified.

The media's power to shape perceptions is profound, and its influence on societal attitudes toward race and morality cannot be underestimated. While white genres emphasize a moral framework and treat infidelity as an exception, black genres often present a narrative where promiscuity and sexual currency are normalized. This contrast underscores the need for more balanced and accurate representations of all racial groups in media, ensuring that art reflects the true diversity and complexity of human experiences rather than enabling reductive and harmful stereotypes.

The unification and improvement of Africa cannot be achieved without first addressing the underlying moral issues within our societies. A crucial aspect of this moral reformation is the establishment of strong family units that foster individuals with a solid ethical foundation. To this end, a significant cultural shift is necessary, particularly concerning the practice of polygamy. Despite being often defended as a traditional cultural practice, polygamy has consistently demonstrated its inefficacy in promoting stable and nurturing family environments. Polygamous families frequently struggle to provide equal attention and guidance to all children. The disparity in parental involvement often leaves many children from such families in situations akin to those experienced by children in single-parent households. This lack of balanced parental care can hinder the development of a robust moral compass and negatively impact the overall upbringing of the children. Therefore, outlawing polygamy is a necessary step towards cultivating family structures that can produce morally strong individuals.

Moreover, the focus on building strong, monogamous family units can have far-reaching benefits for African societies. Such families are more likely to create environments where children receive adequate attention, education, and moral guidance. This, in turn, fosters a generation of individuals who are better equipped to contribute positively to society and uphold ethical standards. By prioritizing the development of strong families, we can lay a solid foundation for broader societal reforms.

Pan-Africanism, Marxist Communism, Socialism, and Democracy, despite their theoretical appeal, fail to address the unique challenges faced by African societies because they are rooted in foreign ideologies. These frameworks, developed in vastly different cultural and historical contexts, often do not align with the specific needs and realities of African communities. One poignant example of this misalignment is the adoption of the feminist movement, another foreign ideology, which has significantly contributed to the erosion of traditional family structures in Africa. The feminist movement, along with its various offshoots like womanism and black feminism, has inadvertently undermined the stability of African family systems. Instead of fostering unity and cooperation, these movements have often led to division and conflict within households. The constant evolution and adaptation of feminist ideologies highlight a recurring issue, Africans tend to adopt foreign concepts and, upon realizing their incompatibility with local contexts, attempt to reshape them through intellectual debates and critical revisions rather than abandoning them altogether. Many African women who embrace feminism often interpret it as a mandate for man-bashing and the pursuit of independence and freedom. However, successful relationships require compromise and the relinquishment of certain freedoms by both men and women. The notion that patriarchy and the oppression of women are inherent to African culture is a misconception. Traditional African societies assigned distinct roles to each member, recognizing the importance and value of everyone's contributions. African societies did not originate concepts such as elections, voting rights, monetary wages, or career roles. These constructs were introduced through colonial influence and have since been integrated into African governance and social systems. However, the imposition of these foreign ideologies often conflicts with indigenous cultural practices and values. To truly address African problems, it is crucial to develop solutions that are rooted in and respectful of African traditions and social structures. Emphasizing indigenous knowledge and cultural heritage can provide more effective and sustainable pathways to progress and unity on the continent.

In conclusion, the path to a united and thriving Africa lies in addressing the moral deficiencies within our societies. Outlawing polygamy and promoting the formation of stable, monogamous families is a critical step in this direction. Only by nurturing individuals with strong moral backbones can we hope to achieve lasting progress and unity across the continent.

9

Standing on Business

In wrapping up, it's clear that the grand vision of a united Africa, free from borders and living in harmonious coexistence, remains a distant dream. Realistically, the continent is unlikely to morph into a single state anytime soon. Instead, progress for Africa lies in a more pragmatic approach: prioritizing nationalism and fostering the development of robust, independent, and self-sustaining nations. The Pan-Africanist dream of a continental union devoid of borders is undeniably ambitious, yet fraught with challenges that may prove insurmountable in the foreseeable future. Africa's diverse cultures, languages, and histories present formidable obstacles to achieving such a lofty ideal. Moreover, entrenched geopolitical rivalries and territorial disputes further complicate the prospect of unity on a continental scale. Considering these realities, a shift in focus towards nationalism emerges as a more viable pathway to progress for Africa. By strengthening individual nations and nurturing their autonomy, Africa can lay the groundwork for sustainable development and prosperity. Building strong, independent countries that prioritize the well-being of their citizens is a more attainable goal than striving for a utopian continental union. Indeed, history has shown that nations thrive when they are united by a common purpose and identity, grounded in a shared sense of nationalism. By fostering national pride and solidarity, Africa can leverage its rich diversity as a source of strength rather than division. Empowering each nation to chart its own course towards progress will ultimately pave the way for a brighter future for the continent.

In the global economic arena, Africa stands as a continent endowed with abundant natural resources and breathtaking climates, assets wanted by nations worldwide. The narrative suggests that with such riches, Africa ought to be a beacon of prosperity and progress.

However, the stark reality reveals a different tale, one marred by systemic imbalances and strategic exploitation. In essence, Africa finds itself at the heart of a rigged game, one engineered to disadvantage the continent and its people. The machinery of this disadvantage is multifaceted, orchestrated to perpetuate dependency and hinder autonomous development. Central to this narrative is the historical and ongoing exploitation by external powers, primarily Western nations, who have strategically manipulated Africa's resources for their own gain. Moreover, the internal dynamics within Africa itself have contributed to this situation. Chronic issues such as intracontinental betrayal, pervasive greed, and a propensity for short-term gains have all played significant roles. These internal fractures have, in many instances, facilitated external exploitation, allowing external actors to capitalize on Africa's internal divisions. The consequences of this rigged game are profound and far-reaching. While Africa possesses the potential for unparalleled prosperity, it remains shackled by a system that perpetuates inequality and stifles progress. The promise of equitable wealth distribution and sustainable development continues to elude the continent, overshadowed by the persistent forces of exploitation and manipulation.

As Africa grapples with the complexities of its reality, the imperative for change becomes ever more pressing. Addressing the structural injustices embedded within the global economic framework, as well as fostering unity and cooperation among African nations, are crucial steps toward reclaiming agency and charting a path towards genuine prosperity. Only through concerted efforts, both internally and externally, can Africa hope to break free from the chains of exploitation.

Achieving true liberation for Africa demands a paradigm shift so radical that many may find it difficult to fathom. It begins with a candid acknowledgment of the rigged game in which the continent finds itself ensnared, a game where the goalposts are incessantly shifted whenever Africa inches closer to prosperity. To break free from this cycle of exploitation, Africa must embark on a path of complete isolation from the global community. This radical departure entails disengagement from international bodies like the UN, the

International Court, and the Commonwealth. Africa must forge its own destiny, free from the constraints imposed by external influences. Central to this vision is the establishment of a sovereign currency, anchored by a gold standard. This entails a return to the traditional use of solid gold and silver coins as legal tender across the continent. Furthermore, Africa must prioritize intracontinental trade and cooperation to foster economic development from within. By trading amongst ourselves and leveraging their abundant resources, African nations can chart a course towards prosperity on their own terms. When engaging with external partners, Africa must negotiate from a position of strength, using its gold reserves as leverage to secure favourable trade terms. This strategy may provoke backlash from the global community. However, Africa must stand firm in defence of its sovereignty and right to self-determination. Even in the face of adversity, choosing to assert its independence will ensure that history remembers Africa not as a continent defeated by external forces, but as a people who dared to challenge the status quo in pursuit of a better future.

10

Conclusion

"You sit in shit too long, it stops smelling. So come the fuck out of there!" **Jenifer Lewis**

www.ingramcontent.com/pod-product-compliance
Lightning Source LLC
Chambersburg PA
CBHW050650250726
48662CB00002B/590